THE
NEW CHAKRA
SYSTEM
HANDBOOK

First published by O Books, 2007
O Books is an imprint of John Hunt Publishing
Ltd., The Bothy, Deershot Lodge, Park Lane,
Ropley, Hants, SO24 0BE, UK
office1@o-books.net
www.o-books.net

Distribution in:

UK and Europe
Orca Book Services
orders@orcabookservices.co.uk
Tel: 01202 665432 Fax: 01202 666219 Int. code
(44)

USA and Canada
NBN
custserv@nbnbooks.com
Tel: 1 800 462 6420 Fax: 1 800 338 4550

Australia and New Zealand
Brumby Books
sales@brumbybooks.com.au
Tel: 61 3 9761 5535 Fax: 61 3 9761 7095

Far East (offices in Singapore, Thailand, Hong
Kong, Taiwan)
Pansing Distribution Pte Ltd
kemal@pansing.com
Tel: 65 6319 9939 Fax: 65 6462 5761

South Africa
Alternative Books
altbook@peterhyde.co.za
Tel: 021 021 555 4027 Fax: 021 447 1430

Text copyright Casey Costello 2007

Design: Stuart Davies

ISBN: 978 1 84694 0

Printed by Chris Fowler International
www.chrisfowler.com

O Books operates a distinctive and ethical publishing philosophy in
all areas of its business, from its global network of authors to
production and worldwide distribution.
This book is produced on FSC certified stock, within ISO14001
standards. The printer plants sufficient trees each year through
the Woodland Trust to absorb the level of emitted carbon in
its production.

THE
NEW CHAKRA SYSTEM HANDBOOK

Casey Costello

BOOKS

Winchester, UK
Washington, USA

CONTENTS

FOREWORD

Being born a sensitive, you could say, is about feeling and seeing things in people and places that most others don't. As a child this, of course, makes you very unsure about what people say and do, usually because you know when they are lying and sometimes what they are thinking. This can be a little frightening at times. Consequently you distance yourself from a person, which in turn confuses and angers them. As a child sensitive you're thought of as a little strange, but as an adult people become very wary.

My gifts were unsettling when I was young, and I pushed them away. As no one gave an explanation of what was happening, I felt my perception must be wrong. Of course, we are all brought up with the fear of ghosts, goblins and nasty monsters that lurk in the dark, so that put an end to my gifts for quite some time – until well into adulthood, when I resided in a foreign country and culture.

I lived on a Caribbean Island, surrounded by a West Indian culture that is a very spiritual, natural, non-materialistic society. In our world we are so wrapped up in what we have, what stuff we own and so on, that often we miss the true meaning of life – learning to respect people for who they are and the type of person they are in the community. Not how much money they have, or the size of their house or the make of their car. So, in this environment, I slowly began to use the gifts again, and to meet other like-minded and sensitive people, realizing that these talents could be developed.

It was during this time that I began to work with the New Chakra System that was channelled during meditations. Eventually I was guided to write this book, so as to make the experience of human evolution open to all.

After many years of working with seven main Chakras (or energy centres), then progressing to thirteen and eventually with the help of

Spirit to fourteen, I came to write this manual. It is a guide to the development of the new human being in company with the expansion of the Chakra System.

It offers an easy-to-understand explanation for all.

BIOGRAPHICAL NOTE

Casey was born in 1956 in Munster, West Germany, to parents serving in the British armed forces. However, the family returned to Britain when she was two. A pretty strawberry blonde, she discovered at an early age that she was a sensitive, one who perceives and is aware of energies not seen by the human eye. She was comfortably able to use a few senses over and above the regular five. She learned that her Grandmother on her mother's side, a greatly loved and respected Cornish woman, was a healer and sensitive, and that she was probably following in her grandmother's footsteps. Though Casey would never say she was a medium, she most certainly is Clairvoyant and a Channel, although through her childhood she found the gifts unwanted and unacknowledged. She was banned from using or being close to electrical equipment such as the family television, as the signal would be disrupted or switches would cease to work; and unfortunately she could not wear a watch as it would continually stop or wind backwards, and would rarely work again. She was constantly aware of the energies around people and would sense their intentions, often claiming out loud that certain people were not nice or had done something terrible at some time.

Some of her childhood was spent in a small village in the New Forest. The late fifties and early sixties were a time of simplicity, and rural life was idyllic, with easy access to the south coast and the small, unspoilt beaches of Hampshire. However, Casey adored the holidays they all spent in Cornwall visiting with the grandparents, who at the time owned a large guesthouse on the North Cornish Coast not far from the town of Bude. It was during these wonderful seaside vacations that she and her siblings became truly connected to nature and particularly the sea: walking along sandy beaches, climbing the rugged cliffs, helping with the farm animals and following her grandmother around the large farm kitchen, making clotted cream and fruit preserves from the berries grown in the gardens surrounding the property.

There was one place that was always a special favourite, the secret garden that her grandmother tended, hidden amongst the rough gorse bushes on the hillside. To arrive at this magical place you followed a steep and narrow path down to a creek that eventually ran to the sea. After reaching the small river, the path led upstream, canopied by sturdy windswept trees and large gorse bushes that arched over the water and protected the walker. Eventually a wooden bridge guided you over the stream and brought you into a hidden and sunny garden. Here were kept the Beehives, sheltered from the cruel salty winds that whipped up from the ocean. Fragrant herbs, exotic fruits and the beautiful flowers that dressed the dining room and reception rooms of the guesthouse were lovingly grown here. For a small child, this world full of delicious smells and vibrant colour offered a freedom to play with nature that opened many windows to the senses.

Casey observed the variety of people who came to sit with her grandmother to talk and ask for help on many levels: some for illnesses, others for guidance and emotional stability. Unfortunately her grandmother never encouraged her granddaughter's gifts or explained what was happening. Perhaps it was the way at that time not to talk about such talents, for fear of causing too much suspicion and alienating a person. However, the holidays were all too quickly over – but there was always the next visit to plan and to look forward to.

Casey put her gifts and extra talents aside, and her teenage years were spent in the City of Winchester, a place steeped in history and ancient sites. The dyslexia that went unrecognized at the time caused her to struggle in her school years, but she battled through the array of subjects and developed an interest in Literature, Science and Art. The sixth form year arrived; and what was she going to do job-wise when she left school? What career was she to pursue? In the early seventies female students were encouraged to go into either teaching, secretarial work or nursing, and no student was helped or advised differently. Casey has a love of films and thought she should combine her interest and skills in art with make-up and work towards becoming a make-up artist for TV and film. Breaking the mould thus caused her teachers much frustration. They gave no help on her future career, but after much research she decided to gain the diplomas in Beauty Therapy required by make-up artists in the film industry. Casey trained in a profession that had not yet become what it is today, and after flunking her interview with the BBC she had to seek work as a Beauty Therapist.

She came to London and spent two years employed by the *Elizabeth Arden's Red Door* salon in New Bond Street as a Beauty Specialist. This was a great training ground for developing people skills, as the clientele of the *Red Door Salon* ranged from regular housewives and workers to the aristocracy and the famous. These skills Casey would use later on when she found herself thrown amongst the rich and famous.

Next, she spread her wings to work on a cruise ship, and thus began her travels. She ventured to the popular and manicured island of Bermuda working as a therapist and aerobics instructor. A year later she returned to London, but was to depart once more, however.

The decision to leave Britain once again was prompted by a car accident that took place on the A1 near the Wetherby roundabout in Yorkshire. Travelling north to visit her mother and stepfather for the weekend, the car she was driving was hit from behind. Her car spun round, hit the crash barrier, then turned and was hit head on by the oncoming traffic. A bad accident, but fortunately she walked away from the crash without a scratch or bruise. Not so the car!

A month before, Casey had been offered a position as therapist for a five-star resort on the small picturesque island of Virgin Gorda, one of the British Virgin Islands, and had actually decided not to take it.

After the car crash, however, she felt she was being pushed to leave, so she departed the capital city to throw herself into a new world. Little did Casey realize how this small island was going to change her and introduce her to a lifestyle most people would die for.

The island of Virgin Gorda is about eight square miles, a long piece of land with a small mountain peak at its centre. It was not developed until the early sixties with the arrival of Laurence Rockefeller who bought much land on Virgin Gorda. Travelling the island was mostly by donkey or on foot at this time, but with the arrival of the wealthy American, a few roads were built and electricity was installed in some areas. The resort of Little Dix Bay was constructed on the site of one of the most beautiful horseshoe bays in the Caribbean. This small island has some of the most spectacular beaches to be found in the region, and fortunately even today they are unspoilt, keeping their natural beauty and wild appearance.

When Casey arrived in the mid-eighties, the island was still relatively untouched, apart from a few expensive and exclusive resorts that attracted the wealthy and important of the United States and Europe who wished to get away from it all, and go unrecognized. The island was a well-kept secret for many years, holding on to its simple, laid-back lifestyle. It could boast three paved roads in the Valley, several streetlights, a small post office, a police station, a clinic, several churches and many bars. The road over the mountain – always referred to as Gorda Peak – had been tarmac a few years before, but travelling was hair-raising and the vehicles driven on the island were mostly trucks, wrangler jeeps and mini-mokes. Island life was slow and simple, the housing basic, mainly small wooden dwellings and a few new cement block houses painted in pastel shades of pink, peach, blue and green with glass louvered windows.

The main town in the Valley is built around the yacht harbour and here could be found the bank, the pub, customs and immigration offices, the yacht chandlery, a grocery store, the Commissary of Little

Dix Bay resort and an assortment of jewellery and clothing stores. This was a far cry from the streets of Central London and for a while Casey found it difficult to understand the island culture and language. But she enjoyed its gentleness and the warmth not just of the climate but also of the local people. On this tiny island the world revolved around Cricket, the yearly Easter Carnival, Christmas celebrations, and the tourist season that stretched from November through to May. But above all it was the natural beauty of the unspoilt countryside that Casey found breathtaking. With the National Park on Gorda peak centre stage, it was a paradise to explore – a true virgin territory.

Virgin Gorda lies on the corner of the Caribbean Archipelago; on one side is the strong dark blue Atlantic and on the other the turquoise warm water of the Caribbean Sea, with long stretches of white sandy beaches contrasting with high rocky cliffs. This area is renowned for sailing, and yachts come from all over the world to meander between these small groups of islands that lie close to the US Virgin Islands, yet which are so totally different. Colourful spinnakers and tall white sails are usually seen on the skyline from any viewpoint overlooking the sea and the Sir Francis Drake Channel. Tortola is the Capital of the BVI and the largest in size; Virgin Gorda, Anegada, Josh Van Dyke, Norman, Salt, Guana and the Camanoes, Necker plus many smaller islands make up the rest of this sparkling chain.

When she was not working, Casey walked the island dressed in shorts and sneakers and plastered in sun cream to protect against the intense heat of the Caribbean sun. She explored the Valley and the village, the old disused copper mine built by the Cornish centuries ago, and the sandy coves and amazing Baths. Huge boulders lying at the water's edge create magical grottos where the turquoise warm tide sends sunlight reflecting on to the huge granite stones. For many a long time, the locals thought that the Jumbies – the bad spirits – lived at the Baths, but slowly realized these great ancient giants were a tourist attraction and began to see a more positive aspect to their existence.

The Gorda Peak National Park is a great treasure of the island only accessible by foot, along small winding trails that lead through tropical undergrowth with a scattering of smaller boulders dressed in moss and lichen. Wild orchids are plentiful in this guarded and rural paradise, and if you're lucky and move silently you may spy the large but shy iguanas that are now protected and no longer hunted for meat by the local people.

It was not unusual for Casey to have a beautiful secluded beach to herself all day, seeing no one and hearing none of the modern sounds. Here was the gentle lapping of the water, the splashing of the pelicans as they dived for fish; a quiet, bright, warm and safe environment, a rare find in a busy world that has no time to stop and reflect. It was a strange existence – one minute she was working in a five star resort with the rich and powerful and all the luxuries it brings, and the next in an untouched natural world and a West Indian Village where time stands still.

Casey began to appreciate where she found herself, knowing there were not too many places in the world where a young Western woman could explore the countryside safely and alone. Her work was demanding and yet the island gave her the opportunity to find a peace and stillness, and above all the time to examine the person she was, to reflect and go within. She spent many hours in the bright, colourful open air, meditating either at the beach or sitting in a secluded part of Gorda Peak and studying the starry mantle that continually sparkled and glowed in the soft velvet nights of the Caribbean. Slowly but surely she allowed her gifts to emerge once more, and this time found them of great service in the profession she had decided upon.

The hotel guests, visitors to the island and friends began sending information and books, and though she lived on a small island far away from the modern world, she was gaining the knowledge she needed. The West Indian Culture accepted and understood her talents more than she actually realized at first, and whenever she could Casey tried to assist the community that had shown her great kindness. Her understanding and perception of energy grew and her desire for knowledge became unquenchable. From feeling energy to seeing energy was a normal part of her everyday life. Her spirituality became a strong force and though she visited and was invited to join many of the Churches on Virgin Gorda, Casey already felt her connection. Channelling energy through her hands was taken for granted, but receiving information and guidance from many levels, this kind of channelling she had not anticipated and at first she was not sure what was happening. She tested the information given, finding everything that was sent from Spirit correct and very powerful. Her personality changed greatly during this time of self discovery, from what appeared to be a typical young woman who demanded the world and all it could offer to a calm, content, unhurried young woman at peace, and with an inner strength acknowledge by everyone.

Casey created a small company with the help and support of island friends and the resorts, becoming an employer, which helped enormously with the increasing workload as Spas and Spa treatments became more and more popular. Not just on the island but worldwide there was a great growth in the Health and Beauty industry in the nineties. Her life driving from one end of Virgin Gorda to the other became hectic, and yet fulfilling on many levels; she enjoyed the island community and the stimulation of meeting and interacting with high-ranked professionals from all over the world. She began visiting her favourite city, San Francisco, at least twice a year, relieving the Rock fever (a negative attitude problem) that can plague islanders or those who do not venture away from the small island environment often enough. San Francisco is a sophisticated city, yet it remains small, quaint and relaxed with a mixed culture. A favourite pastime was driving High Way One north of San Francisco, following the Pacific Coast line of Northern California and absorbing the natural spectacular scenery.

The island of Puerto Rico is a regular stop for the islanders of the Caribbean, its city of San Juan a popular shoppers' paradise; only a forty-five minute flight from Virgin Gorda, it made a great place of escape for a long weekend for Casey. Other cities that became regular shopping and relaxation spots were Miami and Boston.

During this busy time Casey was guided in her meditations to use Thirteen Chakras, and each one was put into place by Spirit. As soon as she developed her energy system her gifts became stronger and more acute, with a great awareness of a larger plan for humans and the earth itself. After keeping this information to herself for at least eight years, at last Casey felt a push to leave her island paradise. It was time to change and to take her information with her, entering the modern world with her new insights and spiritual guidance. It was not an easy decision to make, to depart and leave behind a place that was soft, gentle and surrounded by nature in its purest state; and yet in her mind Casey knew that the island would always be there for her, a sanctuary to replenish her energy and soothe her spirit.

Much to everyone's surprised Casey announced she was leaving and would no longer be working on Virgin Gorda. She was taking a leap of faith, to jump into the unknown, and prayed that a safety net would catch her. She needed to grow not just mentally but spiritually, and now she felt that Virgin Gorda had brought her as far as it could. It was time to move forward; to what, she had no idea. As the months passed, the push she felt grew so intense that it became physical. She knew there was no option but to say farewell to the bright clear turquoise water and warm soft balmy breezes, and the natural energy that had surrounded her for fourteen years.

A few years before, Casey had visited the South of France for the first time. Having travelled all over the world, it seemed strange that a country so close to her homeland should draw her attention, so she made a conscious decision to explore France a little closer. Casey also wanted to expand her knowledge and to study subjects that would be helpful in her work and progress towards the more holistic approach that the world was craving.

It took a year of letting go of her island life, of organizing and saying goodbye for Casey to step on to the plane that would take her back to Britain and a culture with which she had not interacted for many years. Once in Britain, studying and absorbing information, and continuing her meditations, became a priority. But what surprised her was the writing. Her Channel guided her to write the *New Chakra* book to allow others the opportunity to progress. Eventually settling in South Western France, she began writing in earnest, and now continues to write about spiritual subjects and to teach meditation in her new role as a Holistic and Hypnotherapist, delivering workshops on Meditation and Energy.

INTRODUCTION

We interact with a complicated world, finding little balance and peace in our lives. This book will guide you and enable you to find that balance, also providing the tools to gain the relaxation and peace that we all need.

The new human beings that are emerging will be able to understand the personality that they are born with, and the reason for their current lives. We will all feel less out of control and less victims of circumstance. Stress has taken a great toll on our emotions and bodies, but with some knowledge of who we are, the stress will become less pronounced and more controllable.

Being a sensitive and learning to work with a few extra gifts made the world a little easier for me to come to terms with, but we all have this potential and we are all capable of developing these talents.

The book explains the spiritual world as I understand it and have experienced it. Some of the information may have no meaning for you, yet it will give you a guideline to an understanding of the metaphysical. It gives techniques for you to work with your own spirituality, to find who you truly are. Everyone is different, so take from the book what relates to you or sparks your interest.   The meditation exercises will help you to focus and still your busy mind, allowing calm and relaxation to enter your world.

FOR THE EXPANSION OF MAN

For all the people in the world who are seeking their true self – the being they wish to be, the being they once were and the human they are becoming – the way is before you.

Life is eternal, never ending, but continually revolving in a circle of existence.

That we never die on a spiritual level, but move and shift in many human lives to enhance our souls and learn an infinite number of lessons – this it is important to realize, to understand and to believe.

Karma is the collected consequences of our actions during all our human life times since we began this earth adventure.

PART ONE

CHAPTER 1

KARMA

It is now that our science is beginning to perceive with technology what mystics and sensitives have always seen. The American Indians called people who saw auras and other dimensional energies, 'rainbow walkers'. We are all rainbow walkers, not just a special few: all we need to do is to open up and follow some simple rules.

The intention of this book is to give you an understanding of energy dynamics. Your spirituality is your own journey. We work upon the journey on both a human and spiritual level, and our souls progress with the aid of higher spiritual guidance.

Understanding Karma

Always remember: 'we reap what we sow.' If things do not catch up with us in this lifetime, rest assured they will in another. Karma has become a well-used word these days, but how many people take time to understand and make it a part of their lives? This is the first step to change, so let's get to understand karma.

The word means 'the consequences of a person's actions in one life, carried forward to act upon fate in the next; destiny'. Thus, any good you do in this lifetime will come back to you. If you are spiritually attuned, the good will return to you in this life. If you are not, then you will receive good in the next.

Unfortunately, this applies to bad or negative actions and thoughts, too. (Thought is also energy – be very careful about negative thoughts and whom you project them onto!) Such thoughts or actions will return to you tenfold, so think before you do something mean to someone else, even when they have done something mean to you! It could become a continual circle that you and the other person get stuck in, for many lifetimes. The saying 'turn the other cheek' begins to have a real energetic meaning. So, in fact, if someone does something negative to you, do not react but let it go (if possible), so that it remains their karma and does not become part of yours.

Cause and Effect is a phrase we have all heard before. It is related to karma as it means the consequences of our actions. Of course, we all want positive karma, not negative, and the same rules apply – so it is essential that we think and act in a good way. All actions and thoughts create energy, and energy fields surround all things including our selves. Another name for our energy field is the **aura**. Both positive and negative energy stays in our auras and travels with us from one life to another. If you think you have got away with something bad, say a murder or hurting someone – wait! It *will* come back to you and the same *will* be done to you! AH! You cannot get way from karma. You may escape the law of the land, yes, but not your karma.

I am not trying to instil fear into you, but trying to explain what your actions actually do for yourself. We all have choices, deciding which path to follow and the lessons we wish to learn. The soul wants to experience all aspects of the human life, therefore we have all been baddies and goodies; no one is squeaky clean.

Negative Energy

Negative energy is something we all try to avoid, and we certainly don't want it lingering in our auras for lifetime after lifetime. It is found in our thoughts and emotions. Anger, greed and jealousy are all negative, and will stick to us if we are not careful. Anger is a difficult subject to deal with. The dictionary description of anger is 'rage, fierce displeasure, passion excited by a sense of wrong'. There is a saying also: 'what angers you, controls you'. Does that sound familiar? How many times do you get angry and stay in that state for long periods of time and become depressed by the emotion, with a feeling of being brought down? Anger is a dark red colour in the aura, and can make the aura feel heavy and dull, but at the same time very spiky. Anger causes many dramas and can stop you from progressing in your life, from moving forward. If someone produces anger in you they are trying to keep a drama going, thereby controlling your life and your sense of being. The negative energies that surround us can make all our lives difficult and distressing – let it go, and see what happens to your personality and life.

To look upon our enemies as guides is a difficult thing to come to terms with, but without the lessons they bring us in our lifetimes the soul would never progress.

Another big negative energy is Fear. It is like a heavy grey cloud that sits in the aura and can manifest at many levels. Some people live in constant fear, which prevents them from enjoying life. Fear can hold you back from all you ever want, and stop you finding true happiness in a lifetime. We humans have spent so long being afraid of dying; it's our worst fear, yet it is laughably unfounded. We never die, we just move on to other lives, perhaps repeating lessons we got wrong or never finished. Some people touch on their past lives by accident or experience them on a regular basis. Letting go of Fear can change your whole outlook on life, your family, friends and the incidents that take place.

Not forgiving is also negative; it, too, causes problems in our lifetimes. We are so quick and easy to judge others and ourselves, but learning to forgive ourselves is a good place to start. Perhaps we expect too much from ourselves and do not like our weaknesses and insecurities. If we just accept them and forget past mistakes rather than wallow in them, then again life becomes lighter and easier. I'm sorry to say that most of us enjoy wallowing in our negative energies – which is half our difficulty in letting go. They feel safe, we understand them, and anything else would feel unusual and make us vulnerable. Of course, the other problem is that we create negative dramas with other people, or get caught in dramas others have produced in our fight for energy, in order to feed our auras and bodies. That feeling of someone draining you may be exactly what is happening. Non-forgiveness also stays with you from one life to another, and surprisingly it can cause much physical pain in our bodies. So our past can literally control our future.

When we talk of negative energy, the best way to understand this is a force of low vibration and frequency that can be felt by our intuition and emotions, giving us heavy, sad, angry and bitter emotional sensations; our bodies feeling tired, exhausted and unbalanced. 'Out of sync.' is a good expression we use today.

Just imagine negative energies as dark, heavy colours, and positive energies as light, bright colours in our auras – which would you prefer? We all display our karma in our auras, and hopefully we get it cleared by making the right choices: letting go, being brave, putting our best foot forward, and forgiving ourselves and others. Has that helped you, or given you food for thought about your own actions and your relationships with the people close to you and the conflicts that crop up in your life?

The next chapter has to be about energy fields and the aura.

So to conclude with karma, lets say, 'Good Luck!'

CHAPTER 2

ENERGY AND THE CHAKRAS

The ancient tribes of the world and the great religions that have been our foundation stones have spoken of Spirit and energies that surround our world.

Metaphysics is the study of the philosophy concerned with being, and such knowledge of the world that the majority of us do not fully perceive. The terms *Ancient Magic* or *Esoteric* describe the understanding and use of energies that affect our lives, and the vision of other dimensions. Such knowledge has often been looked on with great suspicion. Shamanism has been very prominent in all cultures and demonstrates how the whole world has long been aware that the universe is alive with energies and Spirit. The shaman has long been – and in some cultures still is – an intermediary between man and the metaphysical worlds. Shamans have followed the laws of energy and its rituals, understanding that this is the framework of our being.

So what is all this about?

The Aura

'Energy' is defined in the Oxford Dictionary as 'force, vigour, activity; ability of matter or radiation to do work.' The energy we are considering cannot be measured or seen by the human eye, but can be perceived in many different ways by sensitive and spiritually evolved people. As science has shown, just because we cannot see something does not mean it does not exist. We all experience the human energy field at some time in our life; it can be so subtle and so ordinary most of us don't really consciously register it – for example, having a sense of mistrust about someone, or an instant liking for a person we meet for the first time.

The aura, the field of energy that surrounds each one of us, is different in size, colour and density. It is oscillating at such a fast rate that we cannot see it with our normal vision. All living matter has its own energy field and all energy fields are connected, therefore we are all a part of one another. It is interesting to think and realize that the destruction man reeks upon man and other living things really does affect us all, and particularly the individuals causing the destruction.

We have all heard of the aura, but how many of us have actually seen it? It may be likened to a myth or legend that we read about, whose mysteries only few have seen and understood. There is nothing mysterious about the fields that surround our human bodies, however. They are an important part of living and interacting with the physical and metaphysical worlds. The fields are, in fact, our connection to the spiritual realms. We cannot see them, but they are always there and never leave us. This is a very comforting thing to know, as people often think they are totally alone with no help or love, when in fact it is all around them.

The aura is light vibrating at different speeds, which creates layers around us. The light is made up of many colours, each one resonating at a different frequency; bright colours have a higher frequency than dark colours. If the colours are clear and positive, not negative, dark and heavy, they transcend any pigmented colour that we can see with the human eye. Shining at twilight, they can appear as fairy lights, like the lights on a Christmas tree. Sometimes they appear as a haze or clouds of colour. This may mean little to someone who has never seen an aura or its colours. But one thing is for sure: the aura does not lie. You cannot hide bad feelings and negative deeds in your energy field; you carry them around with you constantly. Energy moves in a spiral, and when negative energy locked in the body is released, it leaves as a dark or black spiral. Positive energy enters the body as white or golden spirals. The healing energies that travel through healers' hands have many colours, and the colours that are needed for each person are given through those hands. We are not a solid mass, but fast oscillating coloured light that betokens energy and gives the appearance of a human form.

The Flow of Energy

Thought is energy. Energy creates. We create our own reality, our own heaven and hell.

Interesting ideas, but they can give us a different twist on life if we follow the meaning. When you feel negative, push the feelings away and do something positive. A good tip is to laugh and smile more often. This shifts and moves the energy in your body, preventing stagnation and negative problems from developing.

Let us consider the energy flowing through and around our bodies. It's not just on the outside. It is very important in keeping us healthy and alive within our human bodies. Perhaps you've experienced the energy moving inside. Some feel it as heat, a vibration, a tingle, a wave, a water sensation, hot or cold. These are all different ways in which people describe their own energy as it moves and shifts. It is changing, shifting all the time; it never stays the same as we move through our lives. The practice of Yoga and Tai Chi and other martial arts helps in moving energy in the body in a positive way, as does the art of meditation.

What happens when the energy gets blocked and movement is sluggish? We can get tired easily, sad and negative, experience physical pain, and draw illnesses to ourselves. Negative emotions and thoughts can be locked into areas of the body, causing the energy flow to slow down and certain areas to become void of the energy they need. If this continues for a long period, a problem can arise in the organ or organs in that region. Rainbow walkers, sensitives and so on see the body as energy, not physical substance. They perceive illness and other problems beginning in the aura, moving into the body and manifesting in an area where energy is not flowing. Therefore, if we can stop the problem in the aura, we can prevent it entering the body and becoming a weakness or sickness. It would be wonderful if we always could, but unfortunately we cannot play God. Our souls may want to experience certain problems and illnesses in order for us to grow and evolve on a spiritual level.

We have energy around us and energy moving within us. The body draws its energy in through centres called Chakras, which are positioned in the aura in the centre of the body, parallel to the spine. They are shaped like spinning vortices, and are sometimes called 'wheels of light'. There are seven main centres. The first Chakra is at the base of the spine; the second is in the sacral region or pelvic area; the third, the solar plexus, is in the area just below the ribs; the fourth is called the heart Chakra and is positioned in the centre of the chest; the fifth is in the centre of the throat; the sixth between the eyebrows; and the last, the seventh Chakra, is situated at the top of the head. They vibrate at different frequencies and resonate with certain colours. It's hard to imagine this is all going on around you and through you all the time, throughout your life. How different life would be and how different we would react to our world if we could all see the energy fields and Chakras! Most of us would be a little choosier about whom we would have around us. It's amazing – we have this whole part of our existence and we don't even see, acknowledge or understand it!

Each layer of the aura is connected with the Chakras. The best way to envisage how they work is as a type of communications network and transformers, reacting to the world around us, receiving information/energy and giving out information/energy, depending on which way the centres are spinning. So if the Chakras are not spinning fast, but slowly, you can imagine that the energy exchange is weak, which is not good for the human body.

The universal energy force that is all around us connects us to each other, to every living thing and to the earth. The earth is also a living being and has its own centres and energy flows. Man is not separate from nature but an important part of nature and the earth. Where did our arrogance come from which allowed us to think we were not a part of nature, but could control it to suit our own needs?

We are not just flesh and blood but emotional, spiritual beings, so these energy centres, or Chakras, work with our emotions and decision-making as well as with our physical bodies.

The second, third, fourth, fifth and sixth centres have corresponding centres at both our back and front: the centres at the back are affected by our 'will' (or what we choose to do), while the ones at the front are affected by our 'feelings and emotions'. Interaction between ourselves, each other and the world around us goes on constantly through these centres, bringing us information and sending information out. If all these centres are healthy and functioning well, we should be well-balanced human beings on every level. Also, our perception of other dimensions should be very acute, enabling us to have greater insight into spiritual matters and a greater understanding of our place in the universe.

However, most humans have an energy system that is constantly breaking down, with Chakras that are not spinning very fast or are closed down totally, and auras with masses of karma-restricting energy movement. This all affects our personality and how we see the world and our relationships with others.

The Meditations

The meditation routines in the book will guide you to sense and balance the energy vortices in your field. There is so much going on around our physical bodies, what with spinning centres, karma and emotional, mental and physical issues, that it is easy to get out of balance. To complicate matters further, we can take on other people's negativity, as it sticks to our aura like glue and can be difficult to shift. Have you ever noticed when you are down or depressed, and bad things happen, they keep on happening? Negativity attracts negativity. Energy has strict laws that cannot be changed and they affect everyone. Life would be a lot easier if we would follow the laws of karma.

The Chakra System

Let's look at these Chakras a little closer. We are told we have seven major ones and about twenty-one minor centres around the 'light body', another name for our field or aura.

This is a guide to help you understand the system and how it interacts with the human body.

The lower three centres, Chakras one, two and three are connected to the physical body while the upper centres are related more to the spiritual levels. Each one also relates to the endocrine system, responding to a certain colour and sound. (Some sensitives do not see colour but work on the sound that each centre resonates). Some believe that the base centre or Chakra one (at the base of the spine) corresponds to the reproductive system, others that it is related to the adrenal glands on the kidneys. I feel equivocal about this.

UNDERSTANDING THE CENTRES

BASE	Red	Adrenals	sound "Am"
SACRAL	Orange	Gonads/ Reproductive system	sound "Vam"
SOLAR PLEXUS	Yellow	Pancreas	sound "Ram"
HEART	Green	Thymus	sound "Lam"
THROAT	Blue	Thyroid	sound "Ham"
BROW	Indigo	Pituitary	sound "Om"
CROWN	Violet /Gold	Pineal	

Illustration
This is just a guide. It is not essential to learn this information unless you plan to be a healer. However, it does offer some knowledge of

 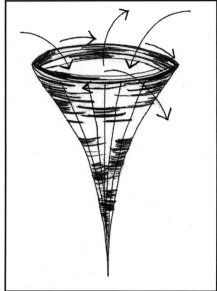

Diagram - The Old Chakra System and a Chakra

how the centres work within our bodies.

Firstly, it is important for everyone to work with the old seven-centre system, before progressing to the new thirteen-centre system; the newer ones cannot be activated until the old ones are working properly and you have reached a level of spirituality that your guides feel is suitable. This is a lesson in patience.

Intention

Intention is your purpose or aim for doing a subject or task. Intention is very important element of energy/Spirit and to use energy and meditation for selfish, greedy or manipulative reasons is foolish and never works. Begin the meditation exercises with a clear and pure purpose and you will find everything will flow easily.

CHAPTER 3

PREPARING FOR MEDITATION

Before you start meditating, you must make sure this is what you want to do. The desire has to be strong and the intent to work with your consciousness and to go within must be pure. Please do not expect wonderful results from your meditations straight away, as it takes a lot of practice to calm the mind and body, to bring it to a standstill, and to listen.

At first the mind finds it tough to stop being busy with thoughts, images and sounds, so do not despair if this is hard to achieve. It is common. Also the body may want to fidget and move around or you may want to fall asleep.

It is important to be in the right position for your meditation, and basically you need to find what suits you. A lot of methods dictate how you should sit, but please do what feels right for you. If you are uncomfortable, the energy will not flow freely, which may hinder your progression.

Your clothing should be loose and warm. Remove any belts, heavy jewellery, scarves and shoes.

Suggested Positions

Sit on a high back chair, with feet firmly and comfortably placed on the ground. The chair must not be too high, nor restrict the blood flow to the legs. Try to have your back and neck straight, but relaxed. You may need to place a pillow or a rolled-up towel behind your neck or in the small of your back for support. Place hands on your thighs, palms facing up or down. Again do what feels comfortable for you, but I find I change the position of my hands during meditation.

There are meditation chairs available, which have high backs and very short legs, so you can sit cross-legged, close to the ground. This might be good if you do not like to sit on the ground. Your back and neck should be straight and relaxed; hands positioned resting on knees, palms either up or down.

For those who like being on the ground, find a good comfortable mat or carpet so there is little pressure on particular areas. Sit cross-legged with back and neck straight, but relaxed. Place hands on your knees as desired. You may need to sit on a pillow or a rolled towel to lift your body up so your legs are comfortable.

Lie flat on the ground or on a firm surface, with a comfortable mat. Support the neck and back as needed with pillows or towels. A support under your knees may be good if you suffer from lower back pain.

Products to Assist your Meditation Time
There are many products on the market these days to assist in relaxation and to help focus the mind inward and to block out external influences.

Have fun trying them out:

Burning essential oils

Applying essential oils to the body, particularly in the areas of the Chakras

Soft music – I find classic music excellent for focusing

Chanting, focusing on a particular word, phrase, sound or note

Coloured lights

Candles (use suitable and safe candle and tea light holders, keep candles at a safe distance from flammable fabrics, objects and your own person and do not leave unattended).

Outside in a natural environment

Burning smug sticks to clear negative energy. (Good to use before a meditation)

Sea Salt added to your bath water. (To use before a meditation)

Energetic sprays, working on the centres

Meditation chairs, pillows and mats
Eye pillow – with or without herbs
Neck pillow – with or without herbs
Crystals and semi precious stones
Feathers

Getting Started

You may find meditation in a class is more beneficial to you rather than being on your own, as it's a little daunting at first. You can also get a group of friends or like-minded people together and see how it goes from there.

Grounding

You have chosen the place, position and products for your meditation, now we need to prepare the body and the body's energies. Before any meditation takes place you must ground yourself. What does this actually mean?

You will hear the word 'ground' often from meditators. We are a circuit of energy and we need to ground the energies to the earth. This enables us to return to a normal state of consciousness after meditation, as a good connection to the earth allows for inward expansion. The physical body is a tool for us to experience life: it is our connection to this earth level, so we must not lose that connection. Therefore we *ground*.

Visualization is the technique used. To ground is very simple once you have decided which is your method. The consciousness can fly and expand, but the physical brings us back to the personality we are. Think of our bodies as an electrical piece of equipment that has to be earthed. Some imagine growing roots from their feet into the earth, allowing the roots to spread out. Others imagine their feet sinking into the earth, or sinking into soft, warm, white sand at the seashore. A very masculine image is to imagine your feet becoming the talons of an eagle or bird of prey, gripping hold of the earth. At first this does feel strange, but slowly with practice you begin to sense the connection to the earth and the safe comfortable feeling it brings.

Protection

After grounding, the next stage is to place a protection field around your aura. This stops unwanted energies attaching to you and disrupting the flow, but it also gives you a sense of security. This again is done with visualization. Imagine a force field around you. It can be any size, shape, colour, thickness you would like. Imagine a beautiful cloak draped around you, for example; this is also a nice easy form to visualize. Thought is energy, energy creates, and you will have your protection in place.

Meditations for the seven-centre system have to be well practised before you are able to move on to the New Chakra System. In other words you cannot jump the gun.

CHAPTER 4

MEDITATIONS FOR THE

SEVEN-CENTRED SYSTEM

First Meditation

To work with moving energy in the physical body:

Once you have prepared your space and your body, grounded yourself, and placed your protection around, you can begin. You may find it easier to continue with your eyes closed, using your eye pillow.

We feel our bodies externally, so to feel the body internally is a little alien to most of us. Begin with your feet and lower legs and sense them in-side. In other words, send your awareness and consciousness to them. If it helps to wiggle your toes and move your ankles, that is fine. Slowly move up the legs and into your pelvic region. How does it feel in-side? Does it feel well, comfortable, happy? Any discomfort or stress, sluggishness or pain? Continue this throughout your body, sending your awareness to every part of yourself, sensing problem areas. The exercise may take a while; do not try to hurry it. You will find it will wind you down, making you feel relaxed. Practice moving your consciousness around the body to different areas and see how different parts of yourself feel. This is a good stress-buster routine at the end of the day or before a meditation.

The next stage is spiralling the earth energy up from the ground, through your body, up the spine and out at the top of the head, into the universe. You may feel a tingle at the top of your head, which seems to be rotating; this is normal and a very good sign. You may not be able to get the spiral too far at first, but don't give up.

What you are doing is perceiving energy moving. One effect is that you may see colours and images on your mind's eye. If you feel comfortable, you can now spiral the universal energy in through the top of your head. This travels down the spine and through the legs and into the ground. You now have two spirals travelling through the body, one moving up and the other moving down. The grounding is still in place, just concentrate on the spirals.

The spirals may have a particular colour or colours, may be thick or thin, warm or cold, shiny or matte or may even sparkle. Each person is different; therefore the spirals are personal to you. They are helping to balance you, giving you more positive energy and relaxing the mind. You will feel a vibration; a tingle on your finger tips and toes as this vibration resonates throughout your body. Do this for as long as you feel is right for you.

When you have finished with your spirals, you need to close down. To do this, firstly stop the flow of energy from above, and then imagine the flow ceasing from below. You are still connected to the earth – grounded. How you stop these spirals is up to you – imagine a switch, like the pull-cord of an electrical light, or imagine shutters of a camera lens closing, etc. Once you feel the spirals stop, open your eyes and stretch, becoming aware of your physical body again and the world around you. When you are ready, sit up or stand up, take some deep breaths and drink a glass of water.

Second Meditation
Begin as before, choosing your place and position for your meditation. Remember to remove jewellery or any article that feels restrictive or tight, and remember to use your grounding and protection techniques every time you meditate. Your grounding will become more intense each time you practise, and your level of awareness will increase. After grounding and protection, start with your spiral from the earth: draw the energy up through the spine and out at the top of the head as before. Bring in the universal energy from above and spiral it down through the spine and into the earth. Focus on your spirals for a while

until you feel comfortable, and sense the tingle of the vibration. In this routine you will use your breath to gain a deeper state of meditation.

There is a pause before breathing in and out. Try to keep your shoulders relaxed and down, and your neck comfortable. As you breathe in your chest will lift and expand, at the same time pushing your stomach out. This allows your breath to fill the lungs totally.

Hold the breath for a count of 3 before releasing and breathing out. Feel the chest relax, and the stomach contracting in, holding to a count of 3 before breathing back in again.

This is a very easy, but powerful meditation. Breathe and relax, taking your time to perfect the exercise.

Once you have a routine, visualize the colour red as you inhale, drawing it in with your breath. Continue with the colour red for as long as it feels comfortable. Work through, drawing in 7 colours, one at a time: Red, Orange, Yellow, Green, Blue, Indigo and Violet. Take your time with these colours; do they feel warm or cold as you inhale? Do not be surprised if your spirals change with the coloured breath. Do not be concerned if you no longer feel or see your spirals, they are still there and will need closing down at the end as before.

For the final part of this meditation, go to a place in your physical body that is stressed, in pain, or is sick, and send the colour you feel you need, or the colour you like to that area.

To finish this meditation, return to your spirals and close them down, as before, starting with the one from above and finishing with the one from below. Stretch your body, open your eyes, and slowly be aware of what is around you. When you are ready, sit up or stand.

Third Meditation

Once you have mastered the last two meditations and feel ready for a more intense focusing, try this meditation using colour for sensing your Chakras (the old seven system). This is a good balancing meditation.

Begin as before: ground; set up your protection; spiral energy up and down; practise the simple breathing technique, staying focused on your breath for a while, until breathing becomes relaxed.

Each of the colours we used before corresponds to one of the seven main centres or Chakras.

Starting with the first Chakra at the base of the spine, take your awareness or consciousness there. We have used the colour red before and this resonates with the first Chakra. Breathe in the colour bright red, but send it to this area, and start to feel the spin of this centre. Does it feel cold, warm and hot? Is it spinning fast, slowly or not at all?

As this first Chakra starts to balance and spin correctly it will generate a lot of heat, so do not be surprised if you begin to sense this heat and a tingle. Also, it may take many meditation sessions to be aware of this centre or to experience any sensations, so please persevere. The next five Chakras will have a centre in the back and front of the body, so expect to feel a sensation in the front and back. You may sense the heat in the back first, but everyone is different.

When you are ready, move to number two, situated between the pubic bone and belly button. The colour here is a bright orange. Send your awareness there, breathe in the colour orange, and send it to the second centre. How is this one feeling? How is it vibrating, spinning etc? If the first is balanced, this one will follow suit after a while.

Heat will appear as this centre begins to spin freely, and again a tingle may be felt.

The next Chakra is at the solar plexus area, and the colour is yellow. Again as before, send your awareness to this centre.

Next is the heart Chakra, which is green and situated in the middle of the chest. Then comes the throat centre, which is blue, followed by the centre at the brow, between the eyes; its colour is indigo. Last is the centre at the top of the head, with the colour violet, though some may experience the colours white or gold.

Once you have reached the seventh centre and have worked with the colour as long as you feel able, go back to your spiral that enters at the top of the head and enjoy the positive energy this brings into your body. You are being energized and balanced. Move back through each Chakra until they feel comfortable. Start with the top centre and work slowly down.

Stop the spirals and focus on your grounding; open your eyes, stretch your body and sit up or stand when you have come back to your environment.

Fourth Meditation
This final Chakra meditation should be done once the other three have been mastered.

Your intent must be pure and honest to allow this meditation to work, with no desire for external power, but a genuine wanting to progress on a spiritual level. With this meditation you are going to open each Chakra in the aura, but when finishing you *must* partially close them down. It is not good to leave them wide open; it could deplete your energy and encourage negative forces into the aura and body.

Begin with grounding and protection. By now this should be quick and easy, and a true connection to the earth will be felt. Get your spirals working and travelling comfortably through your body, so you are connected to the earth and the Source of universal energy.

You can work with your breathing if you wish, but this is not essential; do what feels right for you.

There are two common imaginings of Chakras – a flower, which has petals to open, or a vortex, similar to a tornado shape. Choose the one you relate to, or you might like to develop your own image of your Chakras that enables them to open and close.

Once your breathing is comfortable, send your awareness to the base of your spine. Sense and feel the Chakra. Use your image and visualize this centre opening or becoming wider. If you use the flower image, as you progress up the centres each one has more petals than the last. This may take longer than you imagine, but don't rush. Use the colour corresponding to each centre if it helps. Work through each Chakra – remember that the second, third, fourth, fifth and sixth have one in the front and the back of the body. Once this has been completed, feel the centres spinning and opening, as they balance the body and allow positive energy into the aura.

This is a very powerful meditation. Once all the centres are spinning open and balance takes place, this is a good time to ask for guidance from higher powers on a problem that you are experiencing or a decision you have to make. See what comes. This is your spiritual journey, and the higher powers will guide you.

When you feel ready to finish your meditation, send your awareness to your seventh centre, at the top of your head; visualize this Chakra slowly closing, until only a soft gentle flow of energy is entering. Move down through each centre until the very last. If you find it hard to close the Chakras, relax and ask for help from your spirit guides and they will assist you. Take your time and enjoy the love energy that surrounds you.

Once you have completed closing the Chakras and only a gentle natural flow continues, stop the spirals as before: stretch your body, and become aware of your physical body. Sit or stand when ready. If you still feel light-headed, do a quick grounding exercise.

***

These meditations are simple and positive ways of calming, quieting the mind and energizing and balancing the body. With practice you will be able to sense, feel and hopefully see your centres spinning. These are subtle energies, so be patient and be aware of what is happening inside your body, and the movement of your energy.

***

This first part of the book has dealt with the old Chakra system and easy meditations. Work has to be done with these before the new centres can develop to become operational and function in this lifetime. Also you must live a life free as much as possible of negative Karma. To have a light and clear aura is essential to enable the centres to spin freely and the energy to move through the body.

Part two will help you to develop and access the new Chakras and add them to your aura. I have tried to write the information as it is channelled and hope this will be a guide you can follow, but each one of us has his or her path to follow.

PART TWO

CHAPTER 5

THE THIRTEEN CHAKRAS

Meditation revealed that our energy structure was once very different from its current form; we were formerly rather more inter-dimensional beings. Then one day a book appeared, written by a sensitive, a person very connected to Spirit. The book described us as having thirteen main Chakras, not seven, as all religious and spiritual beliefs teach. With help from spirit guides, the thirteen energy centres were accessed during meditation, confirming the original revelation.

One's first reaction on working with these thirteen Chakras is to become much calmer in oneself, also more positive. There are subtle changes in personality, and also the third eye (as mystics call the ability to see spiritual levels) becomes more acute at all times of the day or night.

This experience with the spiritual is an important step along the path of learning about the expansion of man and the human energy field.

The New Energy System

As we are all at different levels of development, Chakras under the new system may appear to differ a little in size and shape. But one thing common to every one is their power and strength. This is not external power; it is what we call 'authentic power'.

Anyone in your presence will be aware that there is something different about you. They will spend time trying to understand what it is, making comments such as: 'You're so calm, at peace, content, serene and yet so strong and balanced!' People will also enjoy your presence in their space, even if there is no verbal communication. Your nearness will help to balance their energy fields. You will also feel a great difference in the way that all nature responds to you, not just people. You will have a great feeling of knowing and understanding the bigger picture and being a part of everything. As you begin to get comfortable with your new state and energy body, life will have less conflict, and a natural awareness of the good in all people and their place on the earth will develop. We become less judgemental towards one another and especially towards ourselves.

The concept of thirteen Chakras may be new to most people, but once we become aware of them with meditation we will find them very powerful. We have not had these centres for a long time, so it will take some time of practice in our meditations to activate them. They are more advanced than before and they will enable us to open up to more senses in the human body than we realized we had.

However, the new extra Chakras can only spin and be activated if the old seven are working and spinning freely. The new ones are positioned between, and slightly in front of, the old seven, and two of them are located within the aura to the left and right of the head. They spin according to the direction of rotation of the Chakra below them, for example, the new one between the second and fourth centres spins the same way as the second Chakra. The two centres on either side of the head pulsate with many colours, like a kaleidoscope. The colours of the other centres are a combination of those of the Chakras above and below, and extremely bright and radiant. The human aura becomes much wider and very strong. Though the layers are as before, they contain the new colours. The new human being will have the same physical appearance as before, but the energetic body will look and feel a little different.

As we begin to see through the veil that Spirit devised to limit our perception, life will become fuller and more positive. Spirit is eternal, shifting, changing and growing all the time. There are many Sacred Spaces in the world where we can connect easily to the Source (or God), but it depends on our intentions and level of growth as to which areas are suitable. Once we become new humans, these Sacred Spaces will all be open to us for nurturing our personality and Soul. Slowly we will begin to create Sacred Space around us, touching whoever enters that space.

To define Sacred Space: it is a coming together of the love energy on all levels, where there is no judgement or darkness. We will automatically be drawn to earth's areas of sacred space that are important to us.

The old seven centres correspond to the physical body. The new centres, however, correspond with the spiritual levels of ourselves. To become multi-dimensional people, we need to become more spiritual, and this is what the new Chakras will enable us to do.

There is no new Chakra between the first and second, they give us our connection to the earth level, which is therefore becoming less powerful than before. To enable us to move into and perceive higher levels we need much more emphasis on the spiritual.

The third, fifth, seventh and ninth Chakras are new centres between the old ones. However, the twelfth and thirteenth centres spin up above the head, to the left and right. One spins anti-clockwise and the other clockwise.

The first centre is, as before, the base Chakra, which connects us to the earth and its energies. This keeps us joined to our personality and to the world around us. Many theories state that the base Chakra is related to the adrenal glands.

The second is the sacral and deals with our reproduction and sexual energy.

The third is one of the new centres and is involved in the receiving of knowledge in this lifetime from other earth energies.

The fourth is the solar plexus Chakra, which deals with our emotional response to information or knowledge we receive.

The fifth centre lies at the beginning of the sternum bone, and enables us to access the emotions of the past, both of this lifetime and past lives.

The heart centre, or sixth, deals with love emotions of this lifetime and enables love energy from the main Source or God to pass through us.

The seventh is the window to the soul, giving an insight into its wants and needs, and our tasks in this lifetime; its position is the small dip below the throat.

The eighth is the throat centre, which deals with communication with others.

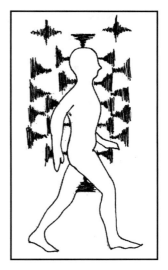

The New Energy System (Diagram Of the New Chakra System)

The ninth is positioned at the mouth and is the connection to our past lives, all the lives we have ever had – these can be numerous.

The tenth centre is our third eye or brow centre, which gives us visual guidance with the energies around us.

The eleventh is at the top of the head and connects us to the main source of energy.

12 & 13. The twelfth and thirteenth centres spin in our aura on the left and right side of our bodies. They are our communication beacons to higher energies, or other beings that guide us in this lifetime and every other lifetime.

The use of thirteen Chakras will enable man to perceive different levels of himself, not limited as before to just one world, but open to many worlds and levels. Once we activate these extra Chakras, our auras become much wider and resonate with more colours than before.

Becoming more spiritual would change the way we conduct our lives and the situations that arise during the course of living. Spiritual is a word a lot of people run from; it conjures up images of the unknown, of things beyond our reach, of God and Power. Writing down the words that you think of when you hear the word 'Spirit' or 'spiritual' can give you an insight into your innermost thoughts and fears.

By supplementing the old system, the new Chakras will create more complete human beings who have compassion for all and insights into the bigger picture.

CHAPTER 6

GETTING TO KNOW THE NEW SYSTEM

Let's separate the new Chakras from the old and look at them a little more closely, at what they have to offer and their meanings.

Centre Three

This is the first new Chakra in the aura, and it rotates the same way as centre two; its colour is a bright orange-yellow. It receives knowledge from many levels and energies for the present personality for this lifetime. When this centre is opened, we receive information about the earth and nature. This includes Nature Spirits and the animal kingdom. At this time the earth needs us to become attuned to its needs, as it too is changing. A strong connection with nature will take place, and the personality will seek ways of preserving the planet and its creatures. Knowledge of how to assist the earth will enter here, and a great joy in life and an appreciation of what is around us will take place.

Communication and a dialogue may begin between the nature spirits and animal consciousness, once this centre is open. Because this centre is near to one and two, the very earthy Chakras, our personal relationships begin to change at a positive level. The way nature reacts to us will be different: there will be more response from animals – they will be drawn to us, while we are drawn to them.

The earth will help us to help it, and a new bond will develop with nature causing a shift in the Earth's frequencies. Earth will be able to destroy the pollutants that man has created, making positive changes in her makeup.

Centre Five

This centre or Chakra lies between the solar plexus and heart centres. It is a very sensitive Chakra as it deals with many emotions from the past, such energy deriving from the beginning of the Soul's lifetimes, which can be far back in the earth's history. The emotions cover the full range and when accessed the person must be balanced and secure in their spirituality to cope with the intensity of the past.

With the new Chakra system, the past and our Karma in many lifetimes becomes important, and the new human will use this as a tool in understanding the dramas that appear in this and other lives. This Chakra will enable us to recognize people from our past lives and understand the energy that needs to be balanced. As we clear past-life drama, energy will become more balanced and we will be less likely to create more drama, thus we will have less Karma in our energy fields. The centre will also deal with letting go of personality issues that appear as we experience every day life.

Centre Seven

This centre lies in the small dip at the base of the neck. It gives us an understanding of the Soul's task or tasks for this lifetime. We have free will and choice on our path to growth. This centre will help us understand our choices but also give us guidance to take the right path. Sometimes we take a detour and make bad choices, which affects the outcome of our lives. This Chakra will give us more insight to our paths, together with the opportunity to complete our life tasks without too many hitches.

What are tasks? These are jobs we all agreed to complete in this lifetime. It may be one or more large tasks our soul has promised to fulfil while on earth. We have our own personal jobs to complete, but we also have a world job to start and finish, which will not only help all mankind but also the other spiritual levels. To make this all a little harder, the personality we are in this lifetime has no idea what the task or tasks are.

Spirit has quite a sense of humour, don't you think? Here we are going about our earth lives trying desperately to understand what is going on, yet we're supposed to do a job we have no knowledge about. Tough to say the least!

So you can see how important accessing this Chakra will be for this and other lifetimes. Our guides will find communication much

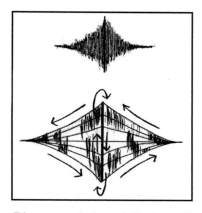

Diagram – design of Chakras 12 & 13

easier at this level, and will be able to give us more support. Unfortunately, they cannot make decisions for us; they can only assist us on our path or paths.

Centre Nine

This new Chakra is situated in front of the mouth, between the throat and third eye Chakras. This one picks up the spin from the throat centre below and its colour is a mixture of blue and indigo. It is the gateway to our past lives, giving us information about who we were and past experiences. Once this is activated a lot of images of long ago will begin to come into our world, different cultures, strange environments that feel familiar but not part of this life. They could appear during sleep, while daydreaming or when in a meditative state. We will recognize them as they emerge into our conscious mind, and in many ways they will feel strangely familiar. This Chakra will give us images of our previous selves but without the emotions that went with the experiences. They will be accessed from the fifth Chakra.

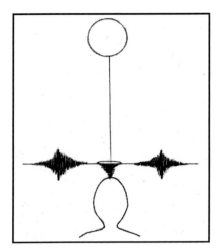

Diagram – Position of the chakras 12 & 13

The Twelfth and Thirteenth Centres

These are out on their own in the sixth layer of the aura, on either side of the head. They are the only Chakras that are not aligned with the others. They spin, one clockwise, the other anti-clockwise. They can alternate their spin when necessary, but they never spin the same way. They are aerials to other dimensions and work like radio receivers to allow communication to take place on a subconscious and conscious level. They pulsate with many colours, which are constantly changing, depending on the frequencies they are picking up.

They are slightly larger than the other Chakras and continue to expand according to a person's spiritual development. At first, as these two centres are activated, they respond slowly, allowing the individual to understand the communications coming through from Spirit on different levels. You can imagine that if these centres responded perfectly straight away it would be too intense – kind of mind-blowing, to say the least, causing great confusions.

When communication is asked for by an individual, a conscious awareness of these centres becomes more apparent, and they can be felt spinning on either side. As communication begins and a connection is made, the energy is received and sent to centre eleven at the top of the head from where it moves down through the Chakra system. A very important part of communication is listening. Spirit must be listened to so that the correct information and dialogue can be established. The meditation exercises in part one will help you to quieten your mind and connect with Spirit – but be patient with yourself.

Do not be afraid to ask for communication from higher levels. It will come in many forms, and when Spirit feels the time is right. Often you can spend weeks asking for help and guidance before it actually arrives. This ability to communicate with other dimensions is for the new human beings who live their lives in accordance with the laws of Spirit. This ability cannot be used for negative reasons or for control, as Spirit will cease communication instantly.

Once your awareness senses the two Chakras, listen to their spin, which resonates at certain frequencies. The different frequencies are different levels of Spirit, or dimensions.

The faster the spin the higher the level of Spirit that is communicating. The two Chakras complement one another and work as one unit. The communication they achieve will continue to develop from lifetime to lifetime. This is important to know, as we become new human beings. Once in place and working, these Chakras will continue to do so for every lifetime we experience from now on. Spirit is there for all of us and these Chakras make everything more accessible.

Once you sense their presence, it's time to tune in. Now Spirit can communicate with you first and not wait for you to initiate the connection. It will become natural to be aware of the spin of these two centres and know when connection is required by Spirit.

CHAPTER 7

MEDITATIONS FOR THE NEW

CHAKRA SYSTEM

These meditations activate and bring light and movement into the new centres.

First Meditation
Begin as before in Part One of the book. Ground yourself, place your protection around you, and get the two spirals spinning through your body, one from the earth and one from above (the universe). When you are comfortable, start at the first centre. Take your consciousness there, at the base of the spine – feel its spin. It may feel warm and radiate heat. And when ready, move to the second centre. Imagine it spinning freely and balanced, feel its warmth, both in the back and front of the body. Move up to the new centre, the new number three. Remember, this one lies between the second and the solar plexus centre, just above the belly button. Focus your consciousness at this point and image a spin; start to feel a heat in the front and the back.

Do not despair if there is little reaction or none at all. It is important, however, that you imagine in your mind that there is a spin. (Thought is energy – energy creates).

Move on to the solar plexus centre, that is now number four. Focus, feel its spin and the heat. Do this at the speed you feel comfortable. Move from the solar plexus to centre five, the next new Chakra at the base of the sternum. Imagine the spin, front and back. Notice any subtle change in temperature here.

Next move on to the heart Chakra, number six. Feel the heat and the spin. Go to centre seven at the dip at the base of the throat, feel the spin and the heat. Centre eight is the throat Chakra. Focus on the spin and heat. The next new centre, number nine, lies at the mouth and back of the head. Feel the spin and heat. Number ten is between the brows and is the last centre to have a front and back. This centre is also called the Third Eye. Eleven is at the top of the head, the old number seven. Feel the spin and heat. Twelve and thirteen lie above the left and right sides of the head. These two spin in alternate directions and no heat may be felt from them.

You have completed the thirteen-Chakra system; finish the meditation by returning to your feet and grounding. Slowly start to move your feet and hands, come back into the room, sit and stand when ready.

This is the first meditation to activate and stimulate your awareness of the new energy system. Expect yourself to change in subtle ways, maybe in your perception of the world around you and how you react in your relationships with the people in your life.

Enjoy the change, which will always be positive and powerful. If you still feel light-headed, do a grounding technique and put your protection around you.

Second Meditation

The Star of Light

Ground, place protection around you, and prepare your spirals. Imagine a star of light above you. It can be any distance away and any size or colour. The star is very bright, shining and light in weight. Imagine the light from this star radiating into centres thirteen and twelve, the two communication beacons, on the left and right of your head and slightly above. Visualize the centres spinning and pulsating with colour. Do not be shocked if you feel their movement in the subtle layers of your aura. Let the light from the star radiate down into centre eleven, at the top of the head. This may give you a jolt sensation, or a feeling of freedom may spread throughout your body.

Move on to the next centre at the brow area; there is a back and front now to all the centres going downwards until centre one. Let the light connect with centre ten as the light passes through from thirteen, twelve and eleven. This makes the energy more powerful so the spin will be faster than you have felt at any time previously. Please relax and know this is normal. Radiate the light through to centre nine. Again, expect a much stronger response than you have experienced before. Carry on to centre eight at the throat, then centre seven at the dip at the base of the throat.

Feel the strong spin and a sensation of being connected to all that is around you. This awareness becomes more definite as you continue down the centres.

Move through six, the heart centre, on to five at the beginning of the sternum bone, then to centre four, the Solar Plexus. Continue on to centre three just above the belly button, and centre two in the pelvic region. You have now reached the last Chakra at the base of the spine.

Allow the light to radiate throughout this centre and down into the earth below.

Enjoy the radiating of the star's light and the wonderful spins of the 13 centres. If you wish to travel to any of the Chakras, allow your consciousness to wander between them. Feel the powerful energy that is generated.

When you are ready, start at number one, work back through each centre and thank the star for its light and activation of each Chakra. They are in place now and will be available to you always and for eternity. Thank the star above and let it leave. Return to your spirals; shut them down, above first, then below. Bring your consciousness to your feet, and ground yourself. When ready, come back to the room.

This exercise has activated the new centres with energy from the Source. You will take a few weeks to feel the full effect of this activation. During the days ahead place a protection around you, especially when in public places.

Third Meditation

This meditation requires the use of the Amethyst stone. Choose one that you favour and use already or one you are drawn to. Amethyst is a very spiritual and gentle stone and has the right vibrations for this exercise.

For this meditation it is best to be sitting either in a chair or crossed legged on the floor. Get comfortable. Place your amethyst stone in front of you, a couple of feet away, on the floor or on a table. With eyes closed, ground, and place protection around you. Just think spirals. Your spirals will already be in place and working, so no need to visualize them unless you feel you want to.

Begin by counting slowly to thirteen – this can be silent or verbal. Repeat a slow count of thirteen three times. On the last count, focus your awareness on the amethyst stone either with eyes open or closed. Sense its presence and vibration, look deep into the stone, and when you are ready, ask it to activate each of the thirteen Chakras.

Start with number one. Feel each centre vibrate with the amethyst before moving on to the next one. When you have finished at number thirteen, thank the amethyst for its help and vibration. Stay still and sense all the centres vibrating at the same time. If you wish to stay focused, send your awareness to twelve and thirteen, feeling their spin and sensing any sounds etc that may be coming from them. These are your communication beacons. Start at thirteen and twelve, work down the centres and gently visualize them spinning balanced and gentle.

When you are ready, return to your spirals and close them down as you have done before. Go to your feet and ground yourself. Come back into the room and gently move.

Keep your amethyst stone with you for a few days as a protection; your vibrations will have changed with this exercise yet again.

Meditation Four

For this exercise you will need thirteen tea light candles, (use suitable tea light holders, keep a safe distance from flammable fabrics, objects and your own person, and do not leave unattended). Sitting in a cross-legged position, place eleven candles in a horizontal line in front with two candles placed six inches on either side of candle eleven, representing the Chakras positions in the aura.

When the candles are lit, get comfortable and begin your grounding, protection and spirals; connect to heaven and earth. At this point, just go back and make sure your protection is strong, or ask Spirit for a stronger protection around you. You are now ready to work with your candles.

Starting from the first candle nearest you, focus on the light and start to breathe in the light. Send this light to your first Chakra. Spend as long as you wish with the light and the base centre. Move to the next candle and the second centre; again breathe in the light, send it to Chakra two.

Move to the third centre, and continue in this way through to the eleventh centre at the top of the head. Chakras twelve and thirteen are to be activated together and must always be treated as a pair. One will not work without the other, without total balance.

Focus on the two candles that represent twelve and thirteen. Let the light become one and blend as you breathe in. Send the light to where the communication centres are spinning and feel the energy created.

Let the light from the candles glow throughout your body and around your aura. If you wish to communicate with Spirit or ask any question to the Source, this would be a good time as channels will be open. You are well protected and only good and loving energy surrounds you.

To finish this exercise, work backwards through the centres and thank the Source and the light from the candles for their help and guidance, visualizing the centres spinning balanced and gentle. After thanking the last candle, close down your spirals and return to your feet and grounding. Begin to move and come back into the room. Blow out your candles and sit quietly for a while until the high-energy calms.

***

I hope you enjoy these meditations and get the response you require. The activation may be immediate or a slow process. Either way Spirit knows and is looking at your Intention.

This is to help us grow and become the next phase in the evolution of humanity. Without the new energy system we will not be able to progress in the new millennium, and as Spirit is waiting for us to take the next great step, start walking!

CHAPTER 8

THE FOURTEENTH CHAKRA

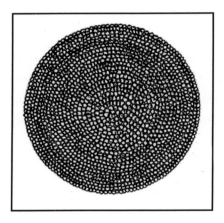

The Diagram of the Fourteenth Chakra (as I perceive it)

Working with the new energy system is a wonderful and powerful experience. Do not be afraid, for if you have come this far, Spirit is there guiding and protecting you.

For a while you will be very conscious of the centres in your energy field, especially centres twelve and thirteen. It is the first time Chakras have been positioned to the right and left of us. These two centres will become larger in size as you become more and more spiritual. Everyone is on his or her own path, so I hope that all this will assist you and give you comfort along your journey of knowing. Just sensing the new system and having a simple understanding will propel you into Spirit's great plan. Things will never be quite the same from now on. Even to pick up this book will change you in a positive and loving way. You could be the meanest, wickedest person on earth, but reading the contents of this book has already started a process you cannot stop. You will never go back, only forward.

It was only after many years of working with the thirteen Chakras and coming to terms with the new gifts that Spirit told me of the last and final part of the new energy system. In fact, it was about eight years. A lot happened in those eight years. Many people had come and gone, and a lot of Karma had been balanced – sometimes very painfully. But not all was bad, since I found that good Karma came back very quickly and profoundly. Having a greater understanding of past-life Karma, and knowing that this was being balanced, I felt as though a great heaviness was being lifted from my shoulders.

It is good Karma to thank other souls for lessons learned and experiences that you have together. Tough to do when it is so painful, but do try it some time, it's very cleansing. Living on a Caribbean island during these eight years was quite an experience, every day thanking the universe for allowing the process to be in such a beautiful and gentle place. It is one of the most natural and quiet places to be tuned in with nature. I hope you are lucky with the place you are in, while going through the spiritual cleanse (a term used for the clearing of Karma). Being close to nature is a great comfort and balancer, as your emotions go to great highs and lows. Yes, the lows are hard, but try and have a support group around you. This is one person or some people that at least can listen. As you progress, like-minded people will be drawn to you and it will get easier: promise! Time is an interesting element and with the new energies it will become more flexible.

Time seems to change, often moving extremely fast or slowly, depending on the situation you are dealing with or the Karma being cleared. Perhaps you have already felt the change in your perception of time, having come this far in the book. It still astounds me how quickly time shifts or stands still when one is unconscious of it. Time has many levels, and for anyone who has lived in a 'mañana' type of world such as the Caribbean, it can become quite fascinating to experience. Time certainly speeds up when you work on spiritual issues in your life, and slows down when you are stuck in a drama. Have fun with time during your process; see how it affects you and all around!

***

Having neither read nor heard anything about this number fourteen centre or where it was situated, the last and final Chakra came as a shock – totally unexpected!

The information about this Chakra was first given to me on a February evening while I was in meditation in central London. There I was, working with the spirals and thirteen Chakras, using the opening up meditation to connect with higher spiritual dimensions, when suddenly Spirit allowed the knowledge through that there are fourteen centres, not thirteen, to complete the system. The fourteenth is a very powerful Chakra, and once activated and opened, it never closes down. This one stays wide open, and all energy from the Source travels through it to reach the other centres.

For about a week after having opened this Chakra, it felt as though a balloon on the end of a long cord was attached to me, floating high above, way out in the cosmos. It was the strangest feeling, as if the balloon was bobbing up and down out in the universe. But this fourteenth Chakra just needs getting used to, and after a while you will find that you no longer feel its presence – unless of course you send your awareness there.

From now on as you meditate, all light and energy will come through the fourteenth centre and work its way down to the other Chakras. Your aura will become extremely wide and it will be able to contract and expand as necessary. For example, in Central London the aura becomes quite small, but once out in the open countryside it becomes wider and very radiant. This is a form of protection, as your vibration is so high and strong with the new system that most people find their auras are a little disorientated. Also, you will be more aware of other energy systems and other people's feelings, which unfortunately aren't always very nice. For a while this can become quite disturbing, and you wonder if the human race deserves the earth that we live upon. But we need the negativity in order to learn. Rest assured that the positive love energy balances all, and has done so since Spirit created our world. Once you become more comfortable with the fourteenth centre you will be able to contract and expand your aura at will.

The next most powerful experience will be your protective shield, or the field that you place around yourself. Your protection can take any form you want; it's how you wish to visualize it. This will come through the fourteenth centre and will be very strong and fast moving. You will be able to use an affirmation to call on your protection. This will become automatic when you feel in danger and uneasy wherever you may be. Your shield is very important for keeping negative and manipulative people and energies at bay. The shield feels as if strong metal walls are being placed around you and it moves very quickly into place. Practise using your shield, and see how fast it moves into position around your aura. It will become stronger and more powerful as you get comfortable with the sensation.

By now you will have become increasingly aware of subtle energies, feeling them, sensing how they affect yourself and others. Do not be surprised if you begin to see them moving within our world; it is quite natural and actually very reassuring. The reality within which we exist will appear very solid and real, and the energies around you will seem so unreal and far removed from your usual sensory understanding. Yet without them we could not exist, and Spirit could not create this amazing playground that is our universe.

Accessing the fourteenth Chakra will change you profoundly, giving you a great sense of the Spirit. Relax with the sensations and do not expect to understand everything at once. The other thirteen Chakras have to be in place and working comfortably before the fourteenth can be opened, otherwise you may have energy overload, too much energy coming through and no way to synthesize it. This is pure love energy from the Source and it will raise your vibrations higher than they have ever been. Try and relax, knowing this would not be happening unless you were ready. It took me eight years to be ready for this powerful input of energy.

At any time you will be able to send your awareness to this Chakra to try and observe it. How does it feel, its vibrations, colours and movements? It feels like an amazing piece of high-tech equipment, but with no sharp edges, spinning very fast, changing colours constantly; a mass of vibration that seems to have a liquid feel about it, yet free-standing in the ether with only one cord attached to it from yourself, like an umbilical cord. At this level it feels as though the soul simply waits and rests. Trust all energy, information and communication that comes through from the fourteenth centre, it's guaranteed to be very profound and pure.

When you feel you may be ready, connecting to this Chakra is simple – but Spirit will show nothing until they feel it is time. In Spirit there is no time. Only on the third dimension do we have the concept of time. Keep working with your spiritual development, living as much as possible in a spiritual way, following the Karmic code and other laws of energy. Do not stop practising opening this Chakra; it may happen when you least expect it. I had no warning of its presence and did not expect this last Chakra, but knowing it exists will help you gain this last and most powerful component of the new energy system.

Now when you meditate, begin by sending your awareness to the fourteenth centre. Bring the energy in through this Chakra first, and then down to the thirteenth and twelfth Chakras.

CHAPTER 9

MEDITATIONS FOR THE

FOURTEENTH CHAKRA

First Meditation

Prepare yourself as before for meditation. Ground, raise your shield/protection and work with your spirals so all energies are in place, and Chakras one to thirteen are in position and spinning freely. Work through each Chakra to open them as you have done before. This gives you a great sense of belonging to everything on this planet and beyond. At first you will need to practise emptying your mind, and being totally still. This is when guidance will come in from the spiritual levels. It may help to focus on the colours and patterns that start to move on your mind's eye, which can become the most beautiful kaleidoscope imaginable. Watch this as a movie screen, as each colour and shape raises your vibrations. Sound may come with this kaleidoscope, ranging from drums, chimes, bells to a single note. Relax more, knowing you are safe and moving closer to the Source.

When you are ready, ask your guides to help you access the last Chakra, the number fourteen that completes the total system. This they will do if you are ready, or they will say no and ask you to continue working on the other thirteen Chakras, as they may not be balanced.

You will know instantly if the last Chakra has been accessed for you. Enjoy the sensation and the empowering feeling that follows its opening. This will be enough for the first time of working with this centre. Close down as before, but remember that the new centre never closes and will from now on remain open for eternity. Partially close down the thirteen centres, stop your spirals and become focused on your grounding again. When finished become aware of your feet and hands. Move them gently and come back into the room and be conscious of all that is around you. Finish your meditation, as you usually like to. The fourteenth centre will be connected to you. Expect that awareness. It can feel like a balloon high above you, for at least two weeks.

Second Meditation

This meditation will become more profound for you if you do your preparation beforehand. Everyone is an individual, different, so work at finding your own preparation ceremony. You may like to do as I do. Often before a major meditation I will prepare my space and body by cleansing the area with sage and cedar oil, or burning the herbs. I will also bathe with sea salt and lavender oil. I use fresh candles for lighting and give a clear and positive affirmation before each candle is lit.

This is a sitting meditation. It should be done on a chair that enables your feet to touch the ground, making the grounding very strong. As you access this last Chakra, it is more and more important that your grounding stays firm.

Once you have completed the grounding and placed your protection/shield around you as you have done many times before, start counting as you have done in past meditation. Count from one to thirteen, slowly, focusing on where each Chakra is, back and front. Sense the heat and vibration at each centre. Twelve and thirteen will feel a little different as they are to the left and right of you, with alternating direction of spin. When you are feeling comfortable and confident that each centre is open and balanced, begin to create in your mind a large spinning ball of light situated out in the cosmos. As you create this connection, visualize or feel the light getting brighter and more powerful, pulsating and spinning. It will automatically be attached to the Source; and from now on all light, energy and guidance will travel from the Source to you through this Chakra.

Feel this energy flowing from the new centre and allow it to move through your body. Stay with the sensation for as long as you can. This fourteenth centre will remain open, as you prepare to close down the other centres. Thank the fourteenth Chakra for opening and begin to partially close the other centres, starting with the thirteenth and moving down to one. Feel each Chakra begin to close like a flower, each one becoming a flower bud. There will still be some movement with these centres but it will be more gentle and calm.

Once this has been completed, close down your spirals if you have also used these, and return to your grounding. Then take your awareness to your feet and hands and begin to move and come back into the room or area you are in. Open your eyes and take a moment before moving and sitting up or standing. It feels very wonderful in a meditative state and can take a while to return back to your body.

Third Meditation

This is the last meditation for the new Chakra system and the fourteenth centre.

For this meditation please find a safe and sacred place outside. This exercise is for total connection with nature and the earth. Let your intuition guide you to your spot. Prepare the place you have chosen, keeping all man-made objects away from the area. Wear natural-fibre clothes if possible, remove any jewellery and your watch. Sit as you wish and make yourself comfortable. Close your eyes, ground yourself, and use your protection to surround your body and aura.

Bring your spirals from below and above into your body and have them moving up and down your spine as you have done before. This is your connection to heaven and earth. If not seen, they can be felt. Just know they are there and spinning.

Count from one to thirteen, visualizing the Chakras opening as you count upwards.

It may take several counts to have all the centres open and balanced. When you feel that the centres are open and you have reached a deep sense of yourself, use the affirmation:

GUIDE ME, HEAL ME, and CONNECT ME.

Repeat this affirmation as many times as you wish. You will become aware of the universe around you, and your spirit guides will help to open the fourteenth centre. Relax and allow the energy to flow through the last, fourteenth centre and feel its strong connection to the Source. Thank your spirit guides for their help and begin to close the other Chakras down. Remember, the fourteenth stays open forever. This you can become aware of any time you wish, by sending your consciousness to it out in the universe. Close the spirals down, be aware of your grounding, and slowly come back to your special place and open your eyes etc. When you feel ready, move and sit up or stand. You will feel a great sense of peace and understanding, and may be a little light-headed for a while. Just keep grounding to remove this sensation.

CHAPTER 10

A NEW WAY AHEAD

The New Energy System will change us profoundly in the way we interact with our world and the spiritual realms – physically, emotionally and mentally. The Earth will benefit greatly by the change in its human keepers, who will also be able to progress and change for the better. Energy/Spirit is the force that allows us to exist, creating our world and our universe. The greatest and strongest energy is the Love energy; the emotion of unconditional love is all-powerful. Thought is energy and energy creates. We can manifest and project a wonderful world if we try and focus on the positive.

The world we know is going through many shifts and changes of vibration and we are all becoming more sensitive to the dimensions we cannot see with our human eyes. Our other senses that have appeared to lie dormant for eons of time are awakening and slowly guiding us to the next level of development. We never stop progressing and evolving energetically, and this enables us to evolve physically. This is a time of great awakening or change – however you perceive it – and we have waited a long time for this moment in our history.

The first part of this book gave you a basic understanding of energy and the old Chakra system. Enjoy working with the meditations for a while, if you have not practised meditating before. They will give you a sense of balance and connect you to Spirit. Learning to focus within you is the key to Spirit and the spiritual realms. If you feel light-headed after meditating, use your usual grounding technique. A meditation is purely personal: spend as much time as you need to find the ways and routines you are comfortable with. This book gives you a starting point, but experiment with what feels right for you.

It was important for newcomers to the concept of energy and the art of meditation to gain a general understanding of the Chakra system that has been in place for such a long time. Unfortunately you cannot access the new system until the old system is balanced and energy is moving freely in your life.

The New Chakras and knowledge about them is for everyone not just a handful of sensitive people. For thousands of years only a few seem to have had an understanding of and information about energy, which they kept secret, so that they could control people and their environment. This can no longer be so, especially with our age of worldwide communication and equal rights for all.

Spirit is happy that it is time for the shift, and that so much information is out there for anyone who wishes to read and learn. Once read, this book will act as a key to a door deep inside you, and a knowing feeling will take place, as though something that was hidden has emerged. You will recognize others that have had the door opened and the veil lifted. It's great when you meet other like-minded people, it really uplifts you and verifies the work of Spirit and its power.

The meditations for the new system are easy, but a little more intense than the previous ones; expect physical sensations and changes in your personality. Every one of us has his or her path to follow and with these meditation exercises life will become much easier and lighter, as you become aware of the bigger picture.

Your **intention** is also important. To send thought with a good, positive and loving purpose is very beneficial to your progress. What is your purpose for meditation? What is your purpose for living? The reasoning behind your actions is always recognized by Spirit, and if there is a selfish, dishonest and mean purpose, expect some repercussions. The new Chakras are for all those humans who have a pure heart and honest intent. If you started life with a negative pattern do not despair, you can still change. Know that you can always change. Forgive yourself and others.

Change is always scary; it is comfortable to be stuck in the same patterns and dramas that we know, even when they serve no purpose for us. Look at your dramas: do they seem to have a continual pattern? Do the type of people that seem to mirror your needs, problems and difficulties surround your life? Stand back from your life and approach it in a different mode from normal. React differently to see just how dynamics and others' responses change.

***

The new Chakras are the right of every human, no matter your background, past, culture or religion. Spirit sees everyone as equal – a comforting thought! Keep working with the meditations for the New System, and know that eventually they will be accessed both by you and by everyone who reads this book. Patience is a tough lesson to learn and it is no different for anyone who wants to use the New System. So don't give up, but try and lead as spiritual a life as possible, following the laws of energy.

Experiencing your own energy flowing can be strange at first; it is very subtle, but it gives you a very comfortable and peaceful feeling. It can feel like heat travelling around your body, a tingle, a wave-like sensation, or a liquid flowing either cold or hot. These are common ways in which we sense energy moving though our bodies. Perhaps you will experience a different one.

The last meditation exercises will open the most powerful of all the Chakras, number fourteen; everything will now travel through this centre to reach the other Chakras. If you feel disconnected from this world once it has been opened, keep grounded and ask for your protection to be placed around you. Grounding can be done at any time, anywhere – just visualize it happening. The physical body of humans will not change with the new system, as the new centres are relating to spiritual growth at this time. But definitely expect your perception to become more acute and a few new senses to appear. Enjoy your own special journey of development and allow this book to become the key to a door leading to the most exciting world you will ever visit.

Good Luck!

AFFIRMATIONS

FOR

MEDITATION

This is a series of affirmations to aid your focus and prepare for meditation at any time you feel ready. These can be spoken out loud or silently spoken within; both methods are powerful and create the right state of mind for drawing positive thoughts and energy to you. The affirmations are used to emphasise your intention to meditate.

THOUGHT IS ENERGY AND ENERGY CREATES

If you prefer to read an affirmation before beginning a meditation, it may be helpful to hold a lit candle out in front of you and focus your eyes on the flame.

GUARDIAN ANGEL
COSMIC LIGHT
THE CRYSTAL ENERGY
ALCHEMY
THE BEGINNING
KARMA
TIME
THE FUTURE
NATURE
LOVE
FORGIVENESS
ANGER

GUARDIAN ANGEL

As I stand before the universe and all existence, I honour the angels
and their profound place among souls.

I call upon the assistance of my Guardian Angel who watches over
me, guiding and protecting for eternity.

To you my magnificent one who agreed in the beginning to stand
watching my every move within this earthly plain,

Guide me now as I ask for the New Energies that are present on this
earth to become a part of my physical and energetic bodies.

Assist now with the transformation.

With gentleness and grace may I too become a
New Human upon this planet?

COSMIC LIGHT

To the light of all existence

That illuminates this earth and the whole universe,

From the beginning of time and beyond,

Give radiance to this planet and every world
that lives within the Cosmic Light.

Empower the infinite worlds and beings in your brilliance.

The cosmic light to aid all humans to
move forward in their evolution,

Shine upon me now

Illuminate my life and soul forever.

THE CRYSTAL ENERGY

I draw upon the energy of the masters, the great ones that have
shaped and nurtured man through the centuries.

The Crystal Energy has brought us to this point in time,

Given as a gift by the universe to
develop and guide humanity.

I stand with my heart open and ready for the
greatest gift of all.

With the power of the crystal energy may I be guided with the
evolution that will change this planet forever?

May this powerful energy pass through me and around me as I
honour the masters, and all the souls and myself.

.

ALCHEMY

My intention is to move forward and to begin the process that will
make this planet a light beacon for the whole universe.

I am ready and willing to be one of first to take the leap.

Our souls have waited for this information

And now I ask for the positioning and activation of the
New Chakras in my Aura.

A Base Human into the New Super Human.

NATURE

I who have a love of Nature and honour our earth,
request nature's guidance.

For now all earth and we are about to begin
the energy transformation,

Not just humans but also this bright and wonderful planet.

May my transformation take place so that
my work with nature can truly begin?

LOVE

A powerful force of the universe,

The Love Energy enables our world to exist
and our souls to grow.

I honour this great force and know that it
flows through me and around me.

Radiating out to all living things,

May its power and gentle strength guide now
through this amazing transformation.

FORGIVENESS

I firstly forgive myself.

I ask the universe to forgive me,

To forgive all sins and negative thoughts that
create imbalance in my life and world,

Clearing negativity from my body and aura.

For those that have caused harm and karma
may they too be forgiven?

I forgive.

THE BEGINNING

I ask to be a part of the beginning,

To be among the first to grow and develop,

To join with all others and make a stand for humanity
within a world that has agreed to transform,

To change in a positive and spiritual way
and to be a light for the beginning.

To begin

To commence

To start

To move forward.

KARMA

The laws of the universe that we all live by,

Unaware or aware,

That allows us to interact in a continuous revolving world.

I ask for my Karma to be cleared in a calm and gentle way
So that I too may move forward and experience what it is
to be a New Human.

The negative karma that I have gathered to myself,
may I be forgiven and forgive.

THE FUTURE

I stand still and draw the future to me.

I listen and hear the future.

I am silent and feel the future approach,

A quiet soft strong movement,

An energy so powerful it will bring only
light into this world and into me.

I am open.

ANGER

Anger – Anger go away.

Leave my mind, my body, and my spirit.

Anger is no longer needed within.

Ancient anger, old anger,
present anger and new anger

Gone for ever.

Freedom,

Freedom for all.

TIME

My Time – Our Time.

To measure movement within our universe

Time is with us

Time is our friend

And time assists us now in the forward
movement of our Being and the World.

GLOSSARY

Affirmation – A word or phrase repeated in order to focus on an intention.

Aura – This is the energy field that surrounds humans (and all living things). It is unseen by most people but is often felt. The energy of the aura vibrates at a very high frequency. It is also known as the Energetic Body or Light Body.

Balance – The complete and equal levels of energy and movement of the Chakras in the body and aura. The human body that is healthy and functioning comfortably in the physical world is in balance.

Centre – A word used for Chakra in the New Age and Western philosophy of the spiritual.

Chakra – A wheel of light, an energy vortex spinning in our aura, the portal that allows energy from the universe to enter our physical body via our aura.

Consciousness – A term used regarding your mental and inner awareness.

Energetic Body/ Light Body – Another name for the aura or energy field.

Energy – The energy referred to in this book is the invisible force all around us that allows the universe and all things within it to exist.

Esoteric – The world of energy and Spirit that most cannot see.

Grounding – An energetic connection to the earth; also a technique used before meditation.

Intention – Your reason for or purpose behind an action or thought.

Kaleidoscope – This refers to the movement and colours of the Chakras, spinning and pulsating with colour. This is the image you see when looking into the top of the vortex.

Karma – Cause and Effect; our actions in this life can affect what happens to us now and in our next reincarnation. It can be positive or negative.

Love Energy – The most powerful of all forces in the universe emanating from the Source, or God.

Meditation – Contemplation; focus on one thought or object. To meditate is to become thoughtful and internally aware.

Metaphysical – Another word for the world of energy and Spirit that surrounds our physical world.

Nature Spirit – A spiritual entity that cares for nature: the trees, flowers, animals etc.

New Chakra System – The use of Fourteen Main Chakras.

Old Chakra System – The use of Seven Main Chakras.

Past Lives – Our soul has been on the earth before and in some cases many times, as different personalities and at different times in the earth's history.

Protection – A shield or force field placed around the aura to prevent unwanted and negative energies affecting our auras and physical bodies

Reincarnation – The soul's rebirth into a new personality after death of the old personality.

Sacred Space – A special area where the love energy and clean pure energy are available.

Sensitive – This refers to a person who has some form of psychic ability; for example, clairvoyance, the ability to see into other dimensions.

Soul – The immortal and spiritual essence of a human being, which is connected to God or the Source.

Spirit – The power source that controls the energy within us and around us.

Spirit Guides – Entities on the spiritual levels that help to guide us through our lives on the earth plane.

Vortex – An area of concentrated energy, as with the Chakras or centres in the aura.

Visualize – To form a mental image, to create a picture on your mind's eye.

RECOMMENDED READING

Gary Zukav, *Seat of the Soul*, Prentice Hall and IBD, 1990

Brian L Weiss, *Many Lives Many Masters*, Piatkus Books, 1988; Time Warner, 1996

Richard Bach, *One*, Pan, 1988/89/94/2001

Richard Bach, *A Bridge Across Forever*, Pan/William Morrow, 1985

Barbara Marciniak, *Bringers of the Dawn*, Bear & Company, 1992

Eric Klein, *The Crystal Stairs: Guide to Ascension*, Oughton House, 1996

Virginia Essene & Sheldon Nidle, *Becoming a Galactic Human*, Spiritual Education Endeavours Publishing, 1995

James Redfield, *The Celestine Prophecy*, Bantam, 1994

**For The New Chakra System CD
and information on Workshops Please visit
www.caseycostello.com**

BOOKS

Back to the Truth
5,000 years of Advaita
Dennis Waite
A wonderful book. Encyclopedic in nature, and destined to become a classic. **James Braha**
Absolutely brilliant...an ease of writing with a water-tight argument outlining the great universal truths. This book will become a modern classic. A milestone in the history of Advaita. **Paula Marvelly**
1905047614 500pp **£19.95 $29.95**

Beyond Photography
Encounters with orbs, angels and mysterious light forms
Katie Hall and John Pickering
The authors invite you to join them on a fascinating quest; a voyage of discovery into the nature of a phenomenon, manifestations of which are shown as being historical and global as well as contemporary and intently personal.
At journey's end you may find yourself a believer, a doubter or simply an intrigued wonderer... Whatever the outcome, the process of journeying is likely prove provocative and stimulating and - as with the mysterious images fleetingly captured by the authors' cameras - inspiring and poten-tially enlightening. **Brian Sibley**, author and broadcaster.
1905047908 272pp 50 b/w photos +8pp colour insert £12.99 $24.95

Don't Get MAD Get Wise
Why no one ever makes you angry, ever!
Mike George
There is a journey we all need to make, from anger, to peace, to forgiveness. Anger always destroys, peace always restores, and

forgiveness always heals. This explains the journey, the steps you can take to make it happen for you.

1905047827 160pp **£7.99 $14.95**

IF You Fall...
It's a new beginning

Karen Darke

Karen Darke's story is about the indomitability of spirit, from one of life's cruel vagaries of fortune to what is insight and inspiration. She has overcome the limitations of paralysis and discovered a life of challenge and adventure that many of us only dream about. It is all about the mind, the spirit and the desire that some of us find, but which all of us possess. **Joe Simpson**, mountaineer and author of *Touching the Void*

1905047886 240pp £9.99 $19.95

Love, Healing and Happiness
Spiritual wisdom for a post-secular era

Larry Culliford

This will become a classic book on spirituality. It is immensely practical and grounded. It mirrors the author's compassion and lays the foundation for a higher understanding of human suffering and hope. Reinhard Kowalski Consultant Clinical Psychologist

1905047916 304pp £10.99 $19.95

A Map to God
Awakening Spiritual Integrity

Susie Anthony

This describes an ancient hermetic pathway, representing a golden thread running through many traditions, which offers all we need to understand and do to actually become our best selves.

1846940443 260pp **£10.99 $21.95**

Punk Science

Inside the mind of God

Manjir Samanta-Laughton

Wow! Punk Science is an extraordinary journey from the microcosm of the atom to the macrocosm of the Universe and all stops in between. Manjir Samanta-Laughton's synthesis of cosmology and consciousness is sheer genius. It is elegant, simple and, as an added bonus, makes great reading. **Dr Bruce H. Lipton**, author of *The Biology of Belief*

1905047932 320pp **£12.95 $22.95**

Rosslyn Revealed

A secret library in stone

Alan Butler

Rosslyn Revealed gets to the bottom of the mystery of the chapel featured in the Da Vinci Code. The results of a lifetime of careful research and study demonstrate that truth really is stranger than fiction; a library of philosophical ideas and mystery rites, that were heresy in their time, have been disguised in the extraordinarily elaborate stone carvings.

1905047924 260pp b/w + colour illustrations **£19.95 $29.95** cl

The Way of Thomas

Nine Insights for Enlightened Living from the Secret Sayings of Jesus

John R. Mabry

What is the real story of early Christianity? Can we find a Jesus that is relevant as a spiritual guide for people today?

These and many other questions are addressed in this popular presentation of the teachings of this mystical Christian text. Includes a reader-friendly version of the gospel.

1846940303 196pp **£10.99 $19.95**

The Way Things Are
A Living Approach to Buddhism
Lama Ole Nydahl

An up-to-date and revised edition of a seminal work in the Diamond Way Buddhist tradition (three times the original length), that makes the timeless wisdom of Buddhism accessible to western audiences. Lama Ole has established more than 450 centres in 43 countries.

1846940427 240pp **£9.99 $19.95**

The 7 Ahas! of Highly Enlightened Souls
How to free yourself from ALL forms of stress
Mike George

7th printing

A very profound, self empowering book. Each page bursting with wisdom and insight. One you will need to read and reread over and over again! Paradigm Shift. I totally love this book, a wonderful nugget of inspiration. **PlanetStarz**

1903816319 128pp 190/135mm **£5.99 $11.95**

God Calling
A Devotional Diary
A. J. Russell

46th printing

"When supply seems to have failed, you must know that it has not done so. But you must look around to see what you can give away. Give away something." One of the best-selling devotional books of all time, with over 6 million copies sold.

1905047428 280pp 135/95mm **£7.99** cl.

US rights sold

The Goddess, the Grail and the Lodge
The Da Vinci code and the real origins of religion
Alan Butler
5th printing
This book rings through with the integrity of sharing time-honoured revelations. As a historical detective, following a golden thread from the great Megalithic cultures, Alan Butler vividly presents a compelling picture of the fight for life of a great secret and one that we simply can't afford to ignore. **Lynn Picknett & Clive Prince**
1903816696 360pp 230/152mm £12.99 $19.95

The Heart of Tantric Sex
A unique guide to love and sexual fulfilment
Diana Richardson
3rd printing
The art of keeping love fresh and new long after the honeymoon is over. Tantra for modern Western lovers adapted in a practical, refreshing and sympathetic way.

   One of the most revolutionary books on sexuality ever written. **Ruth Ostrow**, News Ltd.
1903816378 256pp **£9.99 $14.95**

I Am With You
The best-selling modern inspirational classic
John Woolley
14th printing hardback
Will bring peace and consolation to all who read it. **Cardinal Cormac Murphy-O'Connor**
0853053413 280pp 150x100mm **£9.99** cl
4th printing paperback
1903816998 280pp 150/100mm **£6.99 $12.95**